HOW TO INVEST AND PROFIT FROM THE NIGERIAN REAL ESTATE MARKET

ADAEZE OBIKOYA

TABLE OF CONTENTS

FOREWORD

Real estate investment is one business I have always known to be a money spinner and if done the right way, it could be a reliable source of unending cashflow.

With my years of experience in real estate sales and development in Nigeria, I have seen the good and the bad, the highs and lows, the beautiful and the ugly. There are some steps and decisions I had taken and wished I never took if only I had the right information and knowledge.

I am glad to let you know that with this book you do not have to make any grave errors whilst embarking on your investment journey. This book carefully highlights the basic and important steps that you can take to make the best investment decisions in real estate.

I have known Adaeze Obikoya for over seven (7) years. She is an amiable person with a wonderful personality. Her intelligence and zest for what she does are highly commendable.

Adaeze is very upright in all her dealings, and her dedication and commitment to humanity and her job are laudable. I have watched her tenacity and doggedness in her business dealings for years, and two things that are synonymous with her are "integrity and excellence." Her track record and vast knowledge in real estate sales and customer experience hold no bounds.

Whether as a first-time buyer or an experienced investor, she strives to ensure that the real estate experience is seamless for all her clients. It is safe to say that she knows her onions and has a great approach to clientele and real estate business transactions.

When Adaeze reached out to me to say that she wanted to put her thoughts on real estate to paper, I was sure there is no better person to do this than her.

Be rest assured that the guidelines and investment strategies in this book will open your mind to exciting and endless possibilities.

Ogege Oghenefego Emmanuel
CEO/Founder, Future Xtreme Investment Limited

DEDICATION

I dedicate this book to my parents: late Engr. M.C. Odigili and Mrs. G.A. Odigili, I appreciate your labor of love for our family. The two of you paved the way for us in society by giving us your absolute best.

Engr. M.C. Odigili, though long gone but not forgotten, you hold a special place in my heart. I watched how you rose from every impossibility meant to weigh you down. Your legacy of hard work and dedication remains true to the founding principles of my life.

And to my mother, Mrs. G.A. Odigili, you are the epitome of what I call "subtle strength." A kind that is rare but should be emulated. The way you have filled up the roles of a father and mother in these past years has been incredible. The quest to give your children the absolute best is deeply appreciated. I cherish and honor you!

ACKNOWLEDGEMENTS

I want to use this opportunity to acknowledge God Almighty who inspires me to do exploits in the field of real estate. The awards and accolades are only possible because He kept me alive and gave me hope. Not just hope but the strength and the grace to live a wholesome life. Having to show up daily for myself, family, and friends whilst running a competitive business that is full of tactics could only be possible by God's special grace.

I also acknowledge my family; my very first investors! You all believed in my new career when I "dabbled" into real estate in 2017. Even as a rookie back then, you never withheld your support from me.

To the Odigilis': my mum, Mrs. G.A. Odigili, my siblings; Nduka Odigili, Moses Odigili, Kelvin Odigili, and Gloria Odigili; and my "sisters in-love," Umoh and Grace Odigili, your love and support as a family have been instrumental to my journey.

To my amazing husband: Mr. Mosopefoluwa Obikoya, the very wind beneath my wings. Thank you for helping me soar. For days you would single-handedly care for the girls so I could go on site visits and take on demanding projects. I appreciate your support.

To my darling daughters: Nifemi and Ireoluwa Obikoya, the two of you are the very essence of my being. I love and cherish you.

To my in-laws: the Sagays' and the Obikoyas', you have never made me feel like a daughter-in-law. Instead, you took me as your daughter and have shown me so much love. I appreciate you all!

How could I forget my "soul sisters"? The banters, the love, and the "sisterhood"! You all are the true definition of "women supporting women." I cannot even forget how you all cheered me on when I voiced out that I was authoring this book.

To my mentor and friend: Ogege Fego, you inspire me to be my absolute best. Your achievements in the real estate space are my proof and a daily reminder that I can win in this game too. You are that well of wisdom that I draw from every time. I have learned so much and I keep learning from you. Our conversations are never without scrutiny, chastisement, and profound knowledge. You are a loyal friend. I appreciate you, sir.

To my friend and colleague: Kayode Badejo, we shared platforms where we were privileged to have spoken extensively about the opportunities that abound in real estate. The knowledge I garnered from those conversations inspired some parts of this book. Thank you for always lending a helping hand. You are a force to be reckoned with.

To every real estate developer and realtor group that I have partnered with, and still partnering with, to deliver excellent and quality services to my clients, thank you for providing a great platform to promote this real estate business.

To my editor and publisher: HADAR CREATIONS, the very first time that I checked you out on Instagram after my friend Tosin Ayeni—for whom you had published a book—had referred your service to me, I said to myself, "I'm going to work with you no matter what!" And when we connected, it felt like we had known each other for years. Thank you for putting your absolute best into this project. You outdid yourself.

And lastly, to my clients, both at home and abroad, this is a note of open appreciation to you all. Thank you for entrusting me with your real estate investments. Your belief in me and my brand is never taken for granted. You make it all worth it.

PREFACE

As a child, I was a young dreamer, one who was interested in big and audacious stuff. It is safe to say my dreams were bigger than what my tiny head could comprehend. I guess that early exposure to loads of success stories contributed immensely to such attributes.

Whenever an opportunity to go gift shopping presented itself, I was that child that would go for the biggest gift on the aisle. And no, it was not greed; it was my little way of expressing my "go big or go home" belief.

Then I grew into a young adult! Oh, an opportunity to start chasing all my big dreams, right?! Sadly, right before my very eyes, an unfortunate event occurred. It was an event that blunted my big and audacious dreams!

I lost one of my biggest inspirations: my father! "The man who fueled my dreams and taught me that I could achieve anything if only I set my heart to it and truly work for it. ..."

I am sure you are wondering by now how all of these stories are connected to real estate, right? You know, I had watched a lot of

Nollywood movies whilst growing up, so the only thing that came to my mind when my father died was **SURVIVAL.** How to navigate life and face all the challenges that would come with the reality of his death!

Did we encounter challenges? Yes, we did! So many unthinkable trials and temptations. But amidst all these trials that we faced as a family, we were never **HOMELESS** in that there was never house rent to be paid! Phew!

Now, that was my first encounter with real estate: *"A roof over our heads."* A glimpse of hope and a huge relief off our tiny shoulders. Such relief that comes with having a place to call "home." A place that is ours! A place to hide our heads after the day's work even when we had not earned enough from our collective efforts to survive the next day.

With such hope, my capacity to dream big started to grow again. And this was attributed to the fact that I had shelter, my family never had to squat with anyone, and I did not have to worry about being thrown out into the streets because we were late on rent.

Then, along the line, I got to experience moments where monies received as rental income from our different rental properties saved us during crucial and trying times. Once again, *the power of real estate* played out!

The after-death events that I feared so much were not as ugly as I had thought, and this was because my dad had decided to put some stakes into different real estate opportunities that he had stumbled upon years before his demise. I know life happens and I acknowledge that there are sad cases where families have lost their homes in the event of the sudden death of their breadwinners.

Now, this is not to mock such events or to scare anyone who does not have any real estate investment yet. My story is peculiar to the early lessons that I had learnt from strategic real estate investments, and its sole aim is to expand your mind to the possibilities that it might provide for you and your family eventually.

This book is targeted at broadening your mind to perceive the peculiarities and the strategic investment opportunities that abound in the Nigerian real estate market. Its sole purpose is to ensure that the reader does not leave money on the table when it comes to the opportunities in real estate but takes on the posture of a profitable investor by making only smart investment decisions.

And for savvy investors who are already playing in the field of real estate, the book would expose you to some modern and viable opportunities that could be explored for a bigger and more robust portfolio.

Real estate, as I know it, is beyond just building or renting out a house. If done properly, it could be a game-changer for you irrespective of your age, tribe, or class.

Stay with me as I take you on this fantastic journey into the exciting opportunities that the world of real estate holds.

TESTIMONIALS

Before we head on to the actual scoop, I have curated real-life testimonies of some clients that had entrusted their investments to my care. The success stories that they have recorded in the real estate industry have been instrumental to my brand as a real estate consultant. Their experiences, the possibilities, and the prospects that their investments have delivered, and still delivering, are captured below:

"If real estate investment is done properly, it could be a great channel to create wealth. I have seen my investments yield over 50% return on investment (ROI) in less than 2 years of investing. The current worth of these properties supersedes my expectations. I have known Adaeze Obikoya since 2018. She has been guiding me through several investments since then. I am genuinely happy to have connected with her. She knows her onions, and I highly recommend her any day, anytime."

— Engr. P.O. Akolade.

"I had the pleasure of working with Adaeze Obikoya, a real estate consultant in Nigeria when I was looking to purchase a property. From start to finish, she guided me through the process with ease, professionalism, and expertise. Her knowledge of the local real estate market and her keen eye for detail helped me find the perfect property that fit my budget and investment goals.

Through my experience with Adaeze, I have come to realize that investing in real estate in Nigeria can be incredibly profitable, especially when working with a knowledgeable and experienced consultant. I am impressed with the potential for returns on investment and the stability that comes with investing in real estate. It is clear that Adaeze is enthusiastic about real estate and helping her clients succeed in their investment ventures.

I highly recommend Mrs. Obikoya as a real estate consultant to anyone looking to invest in Nigeria's real estate market. She has exceeded my expectations, and I am confident that she will do the same for anyone who has the pleasure of collaborating with her."

— Barr. Uche Odigili.

"My wife and I started dealing with Adaeze Obikoya about six years ago (that's 2017 to be precise), and it is natural to be skeptical about new business relationships, especially in real estate. We can say it has been a very pleasant and pleasurable experience, and we have no regrets whatsoever. We are simply amazed by the level of commitment of

Adaeze and her team because their work has been highly beneficial and value-adding."

— Mr. Moses & Mrs. Francisca Olasebikan.

"Ada brings distinctive touch and experience to the real estate business. Firstly, she does her research about any property she is handling before introducing it to the client. Secondly, she confers with you to know exactly what your needs are, your purchasing power and availability. Thirdly, she allows you to go and search for information on the property so you can align your findings with all the information that she has provided. Lastly, she follows up with phone calls after purchase and ensures the right documents are given to you.

With all these, you cannot ask for anything less. I will recommend her to anyone seeking to invest in properties as she possesses the right knowledge and expertise."

— Mr. K.K. Alabi.

"Around 2020, I figured I needed to own a 'piece of Lagos' as I have seen Ada's post several times to the extent that it got me uncomfortable if I didn't do something about the information, she was putting out there. Eventually, I expressed an interest in one of the units on instalments, and Ada confirmed that if I were dogged enough, I could do it.

With the correct mental prep from myself and encouragement from Ada, a year went by, and I was done with the payments and promptly allocated to the parcel of land. The follow-up and gentle prodding were all the help I needed from Ada.

With the current events and activities around the property that I had purchased, I know that I have struck a gold mine. Thanks to 'my preferred realtor' for helping me own a slice of Lagos."

— Anonymous.

CHAPTER 1

NOTABLE & HIGHLY SUCCESSFUL REAL ESTATE MOGULS & INVESTORS

"If you're not going to put money in real estate, where else?"

– TAMIR SAPIR

What's real estate without some notable names that have made a wave in the industry?

You have just read life testimonials from some of my clients. It is also important to corroborate these testimonials using some notable and prominent names with which you can relate. Here we identify some phenomenally successful individuals and brands who have made notable success either as real estate investors or developers.

It is noteworthy that most figures quoted in this chapter are only valid as at the publication date of this book, as the monetary worth and value of these business moguls might have increased by the time you might be reading this book.

MCDONALD'S

As of 2023, McDonald's was valued at $216 billion. And the question that comes to mind is, "Are all of these monies made from just selling burgers?" You guessed right, "The answer to that question is a big NO."

With over forty thousand (40,000) outlets worldwide, McDonald's operates only 15% of their outlets in full. Every other outlet operates on a franchise business model.

It is recorded that they operate a real estate market strategy that helps them rake in great profits. And the strategy is "being the landlord to their franchisees." This strategy involves buying commercial properties across the world, leasing them to their franchise, and earning large markups as rental income. Now do not forget that this is a side income alongside the percentage they make from the annual gross sales that their franchise outlets remit.

What a profound money-making strategy!

FEMI OTEDOLA

Femi is an astute Nigerian businessperson, an oil magnate, and a heavy investor in real estate whose current worth, according to a 2022 Forbes record, is about $1.8 billion.

As an oil mogul and a serial businessman, it was recorded that his investment in 182 flats in a high-brow area somewhere in Lagos Nigeria was one of his saving graces when he lost over $480 million as a result of a price crash on the 1 million tons of diesel that he had on the high sea. This happened sometime in 2008 when it was recorded that the price of diesel crashed from $146 to $34. Naira was devalued and the interest rate on the borrowed capital increased very quickly. Part of his bail-out was his investment in the 182 flats, which he later relinquished to offset part of his debt. Once again, real estate to the rescue!

DONALD BREN

With a net worth of $17.4 billion as of 2023, Donald Bren, an American billionaire, is the founder of the Irvine Company; a U.S Real Estate development corporation. He retained his spot as one of the richest real estate billionaires in the United States by overseeing an empire of more than 126 million square feet across Southern California. It is recorded that he owns over 560 office buildings, 125 apartments, and over 97% stake in Manhattan's MetLife Building.

Donald Bren started his career after he built his first house on a $10,000 loan. He started Bren company, a real estate development company that built homes for people. He then went ahead to merge with others to construct and develop the city of Mission Viejo California. He used the proceeds from this business venture to buy the Irvine company alongside other investors.

In 1983, he was named the majority shareholder and was elected chairman. Several years after that, he bought over the entire company and became the sole owner. Ever since then, he has successfully run the Irvine Company which is currently worth $17.4 billion.

KENNEDY OKONKWO

As of 2023, Kennedy Okonkwo was valued at a worth that ranged between $1 million and $5 million. A well-articulated businessperson who had a pretty rough beginning, from being homeless to being taken in by a good Samaritan after he lost his dad. Though his past was unfortunately plagued by a rough beginning, he is currently a major key player in the real estate business in Lagos Nigeria.

The managing director of Nedcomoaks Limited and the chairman of Victoria Crest Homes, a property development company that specializes in property development, consultancy, provision of architectural designs, and construction. A company that focuses on providing housing to the average and middle class in society. Even though it was recorded that he had ventured into some other businesses, his major breakthrough has been attributed to property development and construction.

GRANT CARDONE

Grant Cardone is a sales coach, motivational speaker, and a real estate mogul in America who was worth $600 million as of 2022. Most of his wealth is attributed to the massive real estate empire that he currently owns.

Grant Cardone was not exactly born rich. Having lost his father at an early age, life did not go so smoothly for him. He faced so many challenges growing up. There were cases of him being in and out of school.

His first job as a salesperson earned him a couple of millions which he put into real estate as his first-ever investment. Today, he has spun all of that around and has successfully grown a portfolio that has earned him a title as one of the most well-known real estate gurus worldwide. Such an inspiration!

ALLEN ONYEMA

Allen Onyema, the current chairman of Air Peace, was said to have started off working in a law chamber as a lawyer with a salary of five hundred naira (₦500) in the 'nineties. He later got promoted with a salary increment of two thousand naira (₦2,000).

Whilst working at the law firm, Allen was introduced to real estate by his very good friend. He was presented with an opportunity to sell about four hundred (400) plots of land in a high-brow area in Lagos. He was allowed to determine his profit as his sellers advised him to mark up the prices of the lands. Whatever extra he made from the sales would be his profit. This rare opportunity made him enough profit that he invested back into purchasing about sixty (60) plots from the expanse of land which he was given to sell.

In order not to conflict with his employer, he resigned and went ahead to establish his law firm. From there, it was recorded that he diversified into other businesses and, as of today, he is the chairman of Air Peace, a renowned airline company in Nigeria.

SEAN CONLON

Sean Conlon's story is a remarkably interesting one. He rose from being a janitor to a highly rated millionaire in the United States. Growing up in Ireland was not so smooth as a child. His parents were living on the fringes of society.

Sean Conlon witnessed a time when a bank tried to repossess their home and that taught him early on the need to own a stable roof over his head. When the opportunity presented itself, he headed to the United States.

His first job was as a janitor. When the opportunity to also sell homes presented itself, he took it. Whilst retaining his day job as a janitor, he worked as a realtor at night. He was able to raise funds to deposit for an apartment whilst juggling both jobs.

He continued to work hard until he joined a brokerage firm fully, where his work ethic distinguished him. Gradually, he started buying bits and bits of Chicago. And today, he is the founder of both Conlon & Co.; a real estate boutique firm, and Sussex & Riley; a high-tech real estate firm with hundreds of employees.

NOLA ADETOLA

Nola Adetola is one of the youngest visionary leaders in real estate in Nigeria. A young man in his early thirties who ventured into real estate after he had run several businesses, one of which was his shoe business. He was into the design and manufacturing of shoes. Luck shone on him when he met a man who he marketed shoes to, the man convinced him that if he marketed and sold shoes that well, he could as well market and sell real estate too.

He took the opportunity with which he was presented. He started as a real estate agent and then later went ahead to become a real estate developer. He is currently the founder and CEO of Veritasi, a renowned real estate development company.

Now, what you have just read are stories of some notable key players in real estate who, in one way or the other, have profited immensely from either investing or trading in real estate. Some stumbled into real estate while some deliberately walked into it.

If you are reading this book, take it as a clue that you are being deliberate about your real estate journey, and I would say congratulations are in order because you are one step away from a life-transforming and mind-blowing experience.

REAL ESTATE DEFINITION, TYPES, AND SOME KEY TERMS

"Buy land, they're not making it anymore."

– MARK TWAIN

To understand a thing, it is best believed to be defined and explained!

Oxford Dictionary defines real estate as *"property in the form of land or buildings."* It can further be explained to mean that it is a property that could consist of land, the buildings on it, and every natural resource found on it such as crops and mineral resources.

Real estate transactions and appraisals can be dated as far back as the 1500s when most lands were being acquired mostly for agricultural purposes. Before it was expanded into use for other activities like industrial, commercial, and residential purposes. This helps us to identify the several types of real estate.

James Chen in his article titled "Real Estate: Definition, Types, How to Invest in It" identified real estate to be classified into: Commercial Real Estate, Industrial Real Estate, Residential Real Estate, Agricultural Real Estate, and Special Purpose Real Estate.

COMMERCIAL REAL ESTATE: As the name implies, it is any property that is used exclusively for business. Examples include office spaces, high rises, shopping malls, and lots more.

INDUSTRIAL REAL ESTATE: It is majorly for industrial purposes like manufacturing, storage, production, etc. Typical examples are refineries, silos, fertilizer farms, tank farms, etc.

RESIDENTIAL REAL ESTATE: These are properties used for housing. Examples could be the condos, flats, apartments, and duplexes that we live in.

AGRICULTURAL REAL ESTATE: This is solely for agricultural purposes. This could be farming, animal husbandry, and any activity related to agriculture.

SPECIAL PURPOSE REAL ESTATE: These are properties used by the public for purposes like government cemeteries, government libraries, parks, and lots more.

Real estate in its entirety includes the land, the additions to it, plus its rights which are inherent to its ownership, its modifications, and its usage.

So, whenever the word "real estate" is mentioned, be sure to think beyond your condo or apartment!

SOME REAL ESTATE TERMS AND THEIR MEANING

For better understanding, I will be explaining some key terms in real estate which you might find later in the context of this book, or you might come across as you journey into the world of real estate investment.

REALTOR/REAL ESTATE BROKER/REAL ESTATE AGENT: This is a professional who assists either homeowners or businesses in selling or purchasing any type of real estate that has been mentioned above.

BUYER'S AGENT: A buyer's agent helps in the procurement or purchase of real estate. They advise on the location, pricing, and negotiations. They also scout around for the best properties that match a buyer's request.

SELLER'S AGENT: A seller's agent's duty is similar to the job of a buyer's agent, but the major difference is that he works with a homeowner or a real estate business to sell their property. The seller's agent guides the seller on the best pricing option for their property. He could also advise on modifications to make the property more appealing and the best time to sell such property.

PROPERTY DEVELOPER: A property developer is an individual or entrepreneur who conducts property development. Simply put, they add value to land or property through construction and development.

PLOT: A plot of land in Nigeria is a mapped-out piece of land and, in some cases, can be measured 100ft by 50ft or 120 ft by 60 ft depending on the measurements imbibed by the state.

ACRE: An acre is a rectangular plot of land that measures 4,046 sqm or 43,560sq ft.

HECTARE: A hectare is two and a half acres of land, and it measures 100m by 100m or 10,000sqm

BUNGALOW: A bungalow is a one-floor stand-alone type of house that is fully detached with no stairways.

SEMI-DETACHED BUNGALOW: This is also a one-floor stand-alone house that is without stairways but in this case shares exterior walls with another kind of itself.

DUPLEX: This is a fully detached two-storey house and in most cases consists of a ground floor and suspended reinforced concrete floors. They usually come with two living rooms and bedrooms. Most rooms are ensuite.

SEMI-DETACHED DUPLEX: This is a twin unit of duplexes separated by one common wall.

TERRACE: This is a multi-type of duplexes that shares most exteriors with adjoining walls to other duplexes.

TRIPLEX: This is a modified type of duplex which has stairways that connect three floors. They come as stand-alone in most cases. But this model is now being adopted in the terrace format and as such can be called "triplex terraces."

MAISONETTE: This is a set of rooms usually on two or more storeys, but in this case, they come with separate entrances.

APARTMENT: This is a self-contained housing unit and could be on either one-storey, two-storey or even a three-storey building depending on the structure of the building. And in this case, it could be called a one-bedroom apartment. This could also be built to accommodate more rooms to be further called a two-bedroom apartment or a three-bedroom apartment depending on the number of rooms involved.

SKYSCRAPER: This is a tall building that consists of multiple floors. They can be used as retail spaces, commercial spaces, offices, or residential spaces.

LANDLORD: Oxford Dictionary defines a landlord as a person who rents out land, a building, or an accommodation that he or she owns.

TENANT: This is a person who occupies the land, building, or accommodation let out by a landlord.

RETURN ON INVESTMENT (ROI): This measures the profit obtained from an investment. And in this context, it measures the profit derived from a real estate investment.

EXCISION: This is a process that allows the state government to release portions of lands to indigenous people, settlers, or land developers.

GAZETTE: This is a publication done by the government that captures a parcel of land that has been excised.

TITLE PERFECTION: This is a process that involves the complete transfer of a property's title and ownership from the seller to the buyer.

DEED OF ASSIGNMENT: This is a document that binds a real estate buyer and a seller. This agreement assigns and transfers the ownership of a property from the seller to the buyer.

CERTIFICATE OF OCCUPANCY (C OF O): This is a certificate issued by the government showing that a person has the statutory right of occupancy to a property.

GOVERNOR'S CONSENT: This is an action by the government consenting to a property transaction between a seller and a buyer through a deed of assignment.

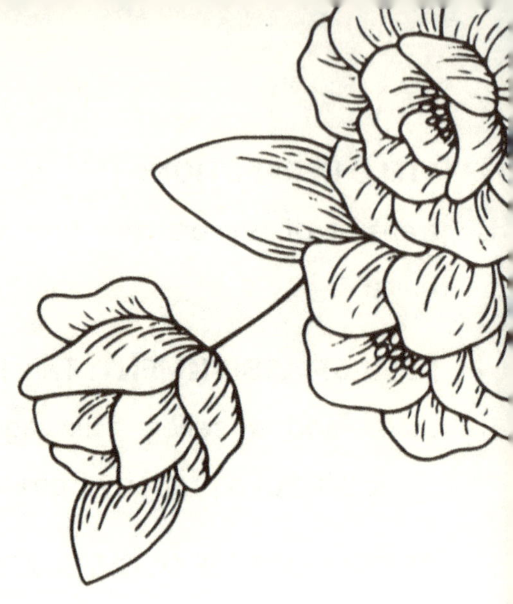

BENEFITS AND THE PROFITABILITY OF REAL ESTATE

> "Landlords grow rich in their sleep
> without working, risking or economizing."
>
> – JOHN STUART MILL

The profitability of real estate is vast and enormous. Apart from its physical features and tangibility, real estate offers great advantages to its owner. The benefits are beyond ROIs and face value. Some of the benefits and advantages are outlined below:

REAL ESTATE PROVIDES STABLE CASH FLOW

Real estate could be a reliable source of passive income. The annual or monthly returns from rental properties are a channel of stable cash flow for her investors. This stable cash flow can be derived from fully built residential houses, commercial properties, or bare land spaces which are put up for lease at a tangible fee.

REAL ESTATE HEDGES MONEY AGAINST INFLATION

The best way to hedge against inflation is to invest in things that have the potential for capital growth whilst retaining their value. Real estate has such potential. It is safe to say that the price of real estate never drops. Situations where a price drop is recorded, for instance, could be a result of distressed sales which are mostly due to emergencies.

Another way the real estate market survives periods of high inflation is the flexibility that allows the price of her rentage to be increased to keep up with the inflation market.

REAL ESTATE IS PREDICTABLE

Real estate is predictable in the sense that, with visible development around a certain location, it is almost inevitable that the properties around such an environment would escape a bloom in price. A typical example is what transpired as a result of Dangote refinery being sited around the Ibeju-Lekki area of Lagos Nigeria. Previously, in 2009/2010, lands around the proposed location for the refinery sold for about five hundred thousand naira (₦500,000).

However, in 2023, the lands around the refinery are currently selling for tens of millions of naira. All of these happened because Dangote refinery was sited at the Ibeju Lekki area of Lagos, resulting in an economic boom of properties in the area.

REAL ESTATE IS SUSTAINABLE

Real estate is highly cushioned and protected from price volatility. Aside from being used as a means to hedge inflation, it could also be used as a means to manage currency depreciation. This characteristic makes it a great contributor to individual, national, and global economic development.

REAL ESTATE GUARANTEES GREAT RETURNS ON INVESTMENT

It is common to see returns on investment in Nigerian real estate go as high as 50% to 100% over a few years. It is like we just wake up to see houses and lands flipped into tons of millions of naira. It should be noted that numerous factors are responsible for this high increase in return on investment. Some of these factors would be discussed at large later on in the course of this book.

REAL ESTATE CAN BE LEVERAGED ON AS A TANGIBLE COLLATERAL

What better collateral to be used for a guaranteed loan than real estate? It is an asset that is largely embraced as a good collateral for a loan either for business start-ups, business expansion, or personal use. The banks and money lenders endorse real estate as incredibly good collateral.

REAL ESTATE CAN BE USED FOR MULTI-PURPOSE FUNCTIONALITY

Real estate, in this context, can be visualized as a piece of land that can serve different purposes at a time. A functional playground with detachable features can be switched to a football pitch, or any desired venture if it is no longer beneficial or serves the original intent or purpose for which it was structured. Bare lands can also be put up for lease over a period for monetary gains until the owner is ready to use them. Eventually, all that needs to be done by the owner is to modify the features to suit the need.

REAL ESTATE CAN BE USED TO DIVERSIFY WEALTH

Whether as an individual, an entrepreneur, or a business owner, real estate can diversify your wealth portfolio. It can be a great "rainy-day" fund investment, especially when you need money to either fund equity or fund emergency needs in one's business or family.

REAL ESTATE IS A TANGIBLE & FIXED ASSET

The intrinsic nature of the physical features of real estate is fixed, tangible, and solid. These features classify it as a real asset. Unlike other investments like stocks which could be lost due to factors like "lack of risk management, overtrading, and poor positioning." Real estate is physical, and it is fixed.

REAL ESTATE CAN BE A RELIABLE LONG-TERM INVESTMENT

Factors like political volatility and capital contributions do not adversely influence the price of real estate. Even though the real estate market fluctuates, it is stable enough to be considered a secure and solid long-term investment.

REAL ESTATE AS A MEANS TO BUILD LEGACY

When you invest in real estate, you are not only investing to generate wealth for yourself, but you are also creating a legacy that can be passed down to generations unborn. This adds to the living legacies that you are already creating either by fighting a cause, running a business, or leading a wholesome life.

REAL ESTATE CAN BE MODIFIED & ENHANCED

Real estate can be modified to suit a current need or could be upgraded to increase its value. A duplex can be modified to a block of flats and apartments if perceived that it would be more beneficial to have it that way. A building can also be pulled down to construct something different. It is imperative to note that once a property is modified, the total labor cost and improvements represent a sizable investment towards that property and as such should contribute to the overall value of the property.

REAL ESTATE CREATES JOB OPPORTUNITIES

Apart from its intrinsic physical feature that enhances the beauty of a place, real estate is known to have given job opportunities to many individuals. On different scopes, real estate has consistently proven to put food on the tables of many people. And this is because it has diverse value chains that involve several types of labor and skill sets. Ranging from the developers, who take on the most capital-intensive part of real estate, to the investors, the engineers, the laborers on site, the retailers, and the real estate agents. At every stage, money exchanges hands, and income is made.

REAL ESTATE IMPROVES THE ECONOMY

Real estate is an indicator that measures the economic growth of an environment. It mirrors the growth and development alongside the poverty level of society. With the enhanced ability to create job opportunities, it is imminent to note its contribution to the economy of society.

The aforementioned points are clear indicators that the benefits of real estate be it economic, financial, or social are limitless. And these benefits could transcend from generation to generation.

It is safe to say that real estate impacts greatly on the progress of individuals, families, communities, and even the nation at large.

FACTORS THAT INFLUENCE REAL ESTATE APPRECIATION

"Property has its duties as well as its rights."

– THOMAS DRUMMOND

Every day we hear about how a property just becomes valued for millions of naira or dollars overnight, but a lot of people are not clear on how these could come about. There are so many key factors that could influence the essential value of real estate. These factors could either be physical, social, or economic. We will be looking at a few factors in this chapter.

LOCATION AND ACCESSIBILITY TO ESSENTIAL ESTABLISHMENTS

One of the most principal factors that determine the price and value of a property is the location. Properties in high-brow locations are highly priced compared to properties in low-brow areas; just the way you get to see properties in towns more prized than properties in villages. This is due to the presence of commercial activities.

Another thing to also note is the property's closeness to prominent landmarks. Landmarks like commercial buildings, markets, schools, shopping malls, and access to major road networks, contribute to the development and value of a property.

STRUCTURE OF THE PROPERTY

The quality of materials used, specifications, durability, and the overall finishing of a house (both interior and exterior) impact on the price of the property in the market. In the same vein, a poorly built house will not attract quality buyers as a result of the poor finishing of the house.

AGE OF PROPERTY

The age of a property can impact its face value. In this part of the world, building designs, architectural designs, and construction activities evolve a lot. What was in vogue years ago cannot be of the same value as what could be in vogue in the nearest future.

Modification is always advised if a property is seen to be outdated. Fixing and enhancing both the interior and exterior of a building, before putting it up for sale, would impact hugely on its selling price. And in situations where it is dilapidated, pulling it all down to construct a more modernized structure might just be the best way to maximize such property.

SIZE OF PROPERTY

The size of a property and its usable space contribute to its worth. The livable spaces and amenities could be a great value-adding factor. A fully detached house in Lekki Phase 1 in Lagos, Nigeria, which has a swimming pool, and a spacious car park is not going to be priced as a two-bedroom apartment in the same environment. Simply put, the better the house type and its amenities, the more highly rated and priced it would become over time.

AMENITIES/FACILITIES WITHIN AN ESTATE

The presence of a gated estate already gives a sense of security. Taking it further by providing constant uninterrupted power supply, a gym area, a sports center, a shopping mall, solar panels, and lots more, assure the occupants a certain caliber of lifestyle. These facilities and their general maintenance tend to influence the outlook of an estate and could further increase the overall value of houses built in such an environment. This should be considered a great appreciation factor, especially for individuals who are considering developing properties to sell on a large scale.

FUTURE DEVELOPMENTS

As a savvy investor, one should keep an eye on areas with plans for future urbanization and commercial developments, especially locations that are close to areas that have been mapped out by the government for municipal projects.

There is a popular quote in real estate that says, *"Go where people are going."* But knowing that Nigeria has her "unique peculiarities," my candid advice would be *"Go where the government is going."* Over time, these areas would attract an influx of investors. It is only wise to strategically position oneself to be a partaker of the potential that such environments hold.

PROPERTY MARKET PERFORMANCE

No matter the aesthetics you put into a building, if the overall performance of real estate in that area is not doing so well, it is expected that the price of that property will not increase beyond a certain market range. The property market performance of a location has an impact on the overall cost and resale value of properties in any society. And this might be influenced by a lack of economic, commercial, or industrial activities in such an environment. This could also be relative to a factor discussed earlier, i.e., "location of the property."

DEVELOPER'S REPUTATION

With a high number of real estate developers flooding the market daily, one thing that stands out is the caliber of developers who have stood the test of time in the real estate space.

Some established names speak of only class and volume. Such developers already have standards that cannot be compromised. At the mention of such names, it is already understood that the properties they would offer would be priced at a certain range due to the "perceived value" of the developer.

DEMAND AND SUPPLY

The demand for real estate is inversely proportional to its supply. When the supply of real estate decreases, especially in highly sought locations, the prices tend to rise, and valuation peaks.

INCREASED POPULATION

A population change, particularly an increased number of persons moving to a location, is a key driver for the high demand for real estate there. This is attributed to the obvious fact that there will be an increase in the demand for a place to stay by the new migrants.

Another great factor that influences high demand is the popularity of a location. The more there is buzz about a location, the more prices of properties in that location are bound to increase.

THE ECONOMY

The universal health of an economy has a significant impact on real estate. An economic downturn in a society negatively affects the value of real estate. The harsh reality is that an economic meltdown would influence homeowners to crash down the prices of their houses or properties to allow for easy disposal. But with a boost in the economy, where a substantial percentage of people are doing well, a peak in pricing would be recorded and properties can be sold effectively and profitably.

GOVERNMENT POLICIES

Government policies provide the structural, social, and legal system to ensure a fair ground for competition in businesses, with the sole objective to promote economic growth. When the policies in place are not favorable to businesses, growth and expansion become stifled. This would further hurt the overall purchasing power of potential investors in real estate.

MONETARY POLICIES AND CREDIBLE MORTGAGE SYSTEMS

If the apex monetary authority in Nigeria can put functional mortgage systems in place and regulate its monetary policies to accommodate low-interest rates on mortgages and house loans, property purchase will be easier. There would be more flexibility and ease when it comes to home ownership as this will encourage more home purchases amongst individuals and investors.

CHAPTER 5

TRIED & TRUE WAYS TO EARN FROM THE NIGERIAN REAL ESTATE

"In my experience, in the real-estate business, past success stories are generally not applicable to new situations. We must continually reinvent ourselves, responding to changing times with innovative new business models."

— AKIRA MORI

Having been around in the real estate space for a long time now, I am privileged to say that I can boldly speak on profitable ways that a savvy investor can consider to maximize profits. This chapter focuses solely on the best approach to ensure maximum profitability from the different investment options that would be discussed.

LAND BANKING/LAND FLIPPING

This is the practice of aggregating plots of land to sell them off in the future. This method has not changed and has been visibly around for centuries. A lot are already involved in this practice, but so many people do not even know. If you have ever bought a piece of land to keep with the sole aim to sell off after some time, then you are practicing land banking.

Profitable Advice

The best posture to take if you want to maximize land banking is to buy on a large scale: in acres or hectares. And not just on a large scale but buy from developing areas.

Buying a plot of land at Lekki Phase 1 for one hundred million naira (₦100,000,000) with the aim to flip is not profitable advice for anyone considering land banking. Rather, it is advisable to take the one hundred million naira (₦100,000,000) to developing areas like Eleko, Ibeju Lekki, or Epe. Buy ten plots of land for ten million naira each (₦10,000,000) or less. Wait for another two years or more, when one plot would be valued at nothing less than twenty million naira (₦20,000,000) or even more.

You would be looking at 100% ROI on a total of ten plots of land. You can then decide to sell off a portion of that land to either acquire more land from a lower terrain or even build a portion of that area that can be put up later for sale. Remember, you still have a portion that you can retain to be flipped/sold in the nearest future.

Now, let us do the math. Your one hundred million naira (₦100,000,000) in Lekki phase 1 could yield you the same 100% ROI, but you are limited to just one plot. And you are only faced with the option to sell off and just walk away with your cash (and that's if land flipping is your only option). But with your investment in developing areas, you have access to more plots of land which can either be retained for future development or flipped for more cash soon. So, this is a case of working with more numbers of plots for more profit.

Bear in mind that Lekki Phase 1 is a fantastic location, especially for commercial or residential constructions, but not in the aspect of land flipping. It would have only made a lot of sense if you were purchasing plots of land in Lekki phase 1 years back when the prices were relatively low.

PROPERTY DEVELOPMENT & CONSTRUCTION

This is often known as real estate development. It involves the construction or improving the face value of lands or properties. It cuts across building new infrastructures on bare lands, renovating an old infrastructure, or converting one building type to another.

For constructions of new infrastructure, an investor can acquire a piece of land, build blocks of apartments, maisonettes, terrace duplexes, semi-detached duplexes, or fully detached duplexes and put them up in the market to either sell or let out, to make profit.

Profitable Advice

If you have any plot of land lying fallow and you can afford some form of development, you should develop to either sell it off or put it up for lease. It depends on what works best in the environment where the land is located. Either way, you would make a good profit. Leasing guarantees stable annual income while outright sale allows you access to bulk money which could be used to venture into other real estate projects.

Now, if you have a fallow land and you cannot afford to develop it, there is what is called a "joint venture." Joint venture is the practice of going into an agreement with another party to develop a project to share both profits and risks that might be encountered. This can be done on either a small or large scale, depending on the number of plots of land involved. You can go into partnership with friends, colleagues, or people in your circle with whom you have common interests.

For an individual with at least three plots of land or more, I would implore you to go into partnership with a "property developer." The reason is that a property developer would know how to effectively manage constructions on that land to optimize profits. You can have land measuring 1,800 sqm and all you are seeing is probably five (5) units of bungalows or terraces. While a developer would take your 1,800 sqm and transform it into twenty (20) units of blocks of one-bedroom, two-bedroom, or even three-bedroom apartments. Let us just say a professional knows best in this regard.

LONG-LEASE RESIDENTIAL RENTALS

This is a typical build/buy and hold strategy where you let out for the long term. This practice is common and is also one of the oldest ways to earn from real estate. Here, there is the usual landlord-tenancy agreement, where the landlord puts the property up for lease and he or she gets paid. And tenants can stay in the properties for years with annual rent being remitted to the property owner.

Profitable Advice

If you are going to engage in this, it is best to build multi-apartments or multiple houses to allow for multiple inflows of cash per time.

Aside from serving as multiple income channels, the landlord gets to minimize loss in case of any unpleasant events.

There have been cases of terrible tenants who would live on a rental property for years without paying their rent. The sad news here is if you have just one apartment for lease and you have such experiences, your effort would be fruitless and it might end in a legal battle, which will eat into your profit margin.

SHORT LETS/SHORT-LEASE INVESTMENT

The short-let business involves renting out a furnished space for a short period. And in most cases, this could be flats, apartments, or duplexes. It also extends to building vacation homes in the form of beach houses and putting them up as vacation rentals on short leases.

This business has gradually gained ground and is seen to be competing strongly with the hotel businesses in Nigeria. As travelers tend to prefer contemporary home settings to regular hotels when they travel or arrive in a new city.

Profitable Advice

The greatest benefit of owning a short-let business is the massive ROI involved. At the very least, a minimum of a six-digit figure is earned per night. And you, as a host, have the sole power to offer the place when you like and also set time durations that your space will be available. If you are not playing in the short-let space as a savvy real estate investor, you are doing yourself a disservice.

Now, let us do some analysis on the earning power of a two-bedroom apartment located at the Ikate axis of Lagos. A typical two-bedroom apartment around this axis on a long lease goes for about three million naira (₦3,000,000) per annum. But on a short lease, you can earn up to seventy thousand naira (₦70,000) per night.

Now, on a 60% occupancy, your annual revenue could be fifteen million three hundred and thirty thousand naira (₦15,330,000). This sum is derived by multiplying the cost per night and the number of days occupied per year (₦70,000 X 219 days, i.e., 60% of 365 days).

Taking away the furnishing cost (which is usually a one-time cost) and the maintenance cost involved, you might just be going home with almost ten million naira (₦10,000,000) per annum. Imagine earning ten million naira (₦10,000,000) per annum on a short lease as against three million naira (₦3,000,000) on a long lease.

From experience, one-bedroom apartments and two-bedroom apartments are highly sought-after for this purpose. So, if you have some plots of land lying fallow in a fantastic location, you might want to consider building blocks of one and two-bedroom apartments for the sole purpose of short-let service. And if you are thinking: "What happens to some of us who do not have the financial capacity to build apartments for these short- let services?" There are options to lease apartments solely for this purpose. But in this case, you would need a special arrangement with the landlord of the property being leased.

It would please you to also note that some factors are at play to run a successful short-let business. The location of the property, the visibility (i.e., advertisements and promotion), facilities in the apartments, the management, and the maintenance of the property are great factors for optimal profitability.

Short lease investments are higher in demand these days in comparison to the typical long lease, especially for people who live in the diaspora with houses back here in Nigeria. Most times instead of leaving their furnished houses to lie fallow, they set it up to make money from it. The fact remains that their houses would always be available for them to use whenever they visit.

OFF-PLAN HOUSING PURCHASE/INVESTMENTS

This is the process of investing or buying a property while it is not yet built, or still being built. In this case, you make a buying decision from either seeing the plan of the house, the 3-D visuals, or an already built-up sample. This methodology is rampant now and is being adopted by most developers as it helps to raise funds from buyers and investors to support an ongoing building project.

On the investors'/buyers' end, it is one flexible way to own or buy a house because the investor is usually offered a flexible payment plan. Payment plans here can span up to 18 to 24 months depending on what the developer has in his or her contract. Eventually, it is a win-win situation for both the investor and the developer.

Note that this option is not for you if you want a house that you desire to move in almost immediately, because most of these houses get delivered within 12 to 24 months depending on the agreement presented on the offer letters.

Profitable Advice

If you do not have the lump sum of money required to purchase a house outright, then this is the best offer to consider. If you are also buying a house to flip in the nearest future, you should consider this too. The reason is, most off-plan houses come heavily discounted.

The developer appreciates your trust in their brand and is willing to compensate the investor with a good offer. You could see a house being offered for forty-five million naira (₦45,000,000) on off-plan but with the sole aim to be sold for fifty-five million naira (₦55,000,000) upon completion. So, you as the off-plan investor/buyer already accrue ten million naira (₦10,000,000) as ROI upon completion.

This can be highly profitable if you are strategic enough to key in at the early stage of the off-plan project as the prices tend to increase as development progresses. The most important thing to note here is the credibility of the developer. Their track record for delivery and how efficient they are as a company should be investigated before making financial commitments. Working with a good agent as a buyer is also important here, as they can point you to the right developer and most importantly the right property.

PROPERTY CO-OWNERSHIP

This is a legal framework that allows two or more people to jointly own or acquire property. Unlike joint ventures, you walk into the purchase of this property together. This has to have very sound legal backing and all parties involved must have their names spelt out on all documents involved.

The biggest advantage of property co-ownership is that it allows for a cut in the purchase price. Individuals involved pay less for a fraction of the real estate. It also allows one to save on maintenance costs as this is shared among all parties involved.

Profitable Advice

This is a wonderful way to earn fractions of real estate especially when one is limited in funds. If you are considering a rental income property and do not want to be burdened by the bourgeois financial load, this could be a great option for you.

Please note that property co-ownership is not limited to rental properties. Co-owners can purchase plots of land together, develop together and put up the property for rent to either earn rental income over some time or sell off after holding the property up for a while.

With co-ownership, one has to be intentional with the documentation, title appropriation, and legal backups. This is to ensure that everyone is up to date with the correct rationing and appropriate fractions that are due to the parties involved.

COMMERCIAL PROPERTY INVESTMENT

A lot has been spoken about residential real estate investment. Here we dwell on how to invest and profit from commercial real estate. This could involve building or buying properties strictly for commercial use. One can earn from commercial properties either on a monthly or annual basis. This depends on the agreement on ground and the type of commercial activity such space is being used for.

Profitable Advice

Properties that are on the major roads, or have proximity or connectivity to the major roads, would be great for commercial use. If you happen to have bare land in areas like this, you should consider building blocks of shops, malls, or high-rise office buildings depending on your financial capacity.

In situations where one cannot afford to build, one can also purchase already-built units. And this does not mean purchasing the whole block. Purchases can be in units and bits. This could be a reliable source of income in the long run.

Also, bear in mind that commercial use goes beyond shopping complexes or malls. A great commercial use could be an event space or entertainment center. Places like Lagos have a high record for partying every other week. If you position yourself strategically, you might be cashing out every weekend.

And if you are not interested in running an entertainment or an event center, your case could be you possess a bare piece of land in a strategic place that can be put up on lease for such type of business. You retain the land while they run their businesses strictly on lease.

REAL ESTATE CASHBACK TRADING

This practice involves investing in real estate projects with the aim of getting one's capital and a percentage of interest back after a certain period.

It is a trading initiative that allows investors to be partakers in the acquisition and development of a large piece of land. This investment is usually backed up with a deed of agreement, a receipt of payment, and a post-dated cheque. In some situations, the agreement could also contain a fraction of the estate in case the company defaults on repayment. Now, it is evident that this option is subject to the agreement being offered by the company.

Profitable Advice

Real estate cashback is new and lots of people are buying into this form of investment. It is also one of the cheapest ways to partake in real estate investment. One can key in with as low as five hundred thousand naira (₦500,000) to earn up to 25% to 30% ROI per annum.

Yet, it is only advised that an investor does his or her due diligence and investigations before embarking on this. This is largely because this particular investment option is new, and the success rate has not been fully determined.

Whichever strategy you choose to adopt, be sure to note that the profits and gains from real estate are not immediate; an investor should allow some time before profits can be recorded. See real estate as sowing and reaping. There is a time to sow and time to nurture before you finally reap.

It is noteworthy that most figures quoted in this chapter are only valid at the time of its publication date, as the monetary value quoted might have increased at the time that you get to read this book.

*It is also advised that every potential investor should actively carry out **due diligence** on any offers on the investment options highlighted before making commitments.*

CHAPTER 6

GUIDELINES FOR INVESTING RIGHT IN REAL ESTATE

"Wise spending is part of wise investing.
And it is never too late to start."

– RHONDA KATZ

You have seen how profitable real estate can be, especially with strategic positioning. However, real estate is diverse and porous. It could be highly vulnerable to fraud, especially in this part of the world. In this chapter, more light will be shed on the appropriate measures to take while getting involved in any real estate transaction in Nigeria at large.

RESEARCH

The first piece of advice is "research." Research expands your knowledge base and guides your decision-making when it comes to buying real estate.

The research starts with you and what you intend to achieve from the real estate market. This is because what you buy is driven by your "whys." You ought to commence by asking yourself these few questions: **"What do I want to invest in? Is it land, a house, or a commercial building?"**

If you are settling for land, then you go ahead to ask yourself:

- "Why do I want to buy this land?

- "Do I intend to build on it, let it out, or flip it for more income?"

- "Do I want the land for residential or commercial purposes?"

- "What location should I be looking at?"

- "Are there landmarks around this property that can influence its value in the long run?"

- "How much tax or land use charge would this land attract in the long run?"

- "What title does this land hold?"

- "Would I be required to perfect the title documents in the long run?"

- "If yes, how much more, am I willing to spend on title perfection?"

And if settling for a house, you go ahead to ask yourself:

- "Why do I want to buy a house? Do I want to live in it, rent it out, or sell it off eventually?"

- "What house type should I consider?"

- "Are there landmarks around the property that can influence the property value in the long run?"

- "Does this type of house fit my current lifestyle if I'm to live in it?"

- "Would I be allowed to remodel the house if the need arises?"

- "What features does the house possess?"

- "Can the features and amenities influence its value over time?"

- "Can this type of house be easily flipped when I'm ready to sell?"

Research should also extend to who you're buying the property from; the credibility of the family/person or the developer that you're buying from; the track record of the developer or the seller involved; the history of the property you're settling for; the title of the property; the documentations involved; and lots more.

HAVE A BUDGET

To get anything effectively done, the number one rule is to "prepare" for it. Having a budget allows you to plan. Why? Real estate transactions can be expensive, so you do not want to walk into it unprepared. The right questions to ask yourself could be:

- "How much am I willing to spend to purchase this property?"

- "Do I have the capacity to pay outrightly for this property?"

- "Do I have the financial capacity to commit to a long-term payment plan if I'm given that option?"

- "How much am I capable of paying as a monthly commitment especially if I'm to opt for a long-term payment option?"

And if you are not financially ready to commit to a property yet, then make plans to finance one.

There are different financing options you can explore: it could be a saving strategy, a loan, or a mortgage scheme. Whichever financing strategy you settle for, planning is still necessary.

ENGAGE THE SERVICES OF A SEASONED REALTOR

When buying, selling, or renting a piece of real estate, it is never advised to work alone. Some skilled professionals are there to help you with these services.

Aside from the technical expertise on getting transactions done, there are several questions that you do not have answers to yet, and this is where a realtor or a real estate consultant comes in. Their job role revolves around comparative market analysis, property inspections, and real estate paperwork. They could also play intermediate roles in negotiation processes and give general guidance on the best locations or best developers to engage with.

The next question that might be on your mind is: "How do I locate a good realtor?"

Note that it is the delight of any savvy realtor to work solely to protect your interest and to guide you through a seamless buying or selling experience. The utmost goal is to find a realtor that has your best interest at heart. And the best way to find one is to ask to be referred.

Seek people and individuals who have successfully achieved the results that you are looking for in real estate.

Having done your research as discussed earlier, it is believed that you are now better equipped with the right information on what you desire from real estate. Spotting a good realtor would be easy because they would have the right answers to your unanswered questions.

GO ON INSPECTIONS

This is mostly for people who are looking to buy or invest in real estate and not people who are looking to sell. Part of the knowledge required to make an informed buying decision is inspection. Schedule site inspection visits with your realtor. Commit time and effort to inspect different properties until you are satisfied.

If you are in the diaspora or live far from the location that you are looking to buy, then you might engage the services of a trusted family member or a friend. One whose intellect and judgment in matters related to real estate you trust.

Technology has also made things much easier these days. Video calls and Google Maps could be effective tools to aid your inspections. From records, so many real estate transactions have been closed through virtual inspections, especially with clients and investors that are based in the diaspora.

CONDUCT A SEARCH ON THE PROPERTY

Having seen a piece of land or a house that you like, the next step is to "conduct a search"! Your search starts by sighting the documents involved. Request to see every document that they claim the property has. If you are not sure what to ask for, your realtor can step in here. Remember that your realtor can only guide and advise you based on the knowledge presented to him or her. But the duty to ascertain the authenticity of a property is still your call.

Conducting a search is not as difficult as it sounds. Aside from sighting the documents as earlier stated, you can take it further by taking site coordinates to authenticate titles and collaborate the presented documents with government policies or mandates. Because of the technicalities that might be involved, it is advisable to also seek the services of a surveyor and a real estate lawyer to help with this quest.

SEEK TO UNDERSTAND THE CONTRACT INVOLVED

A house or land purchase, especially from property developers, usually involves a contract. Seek to understand what is expected of you in that contract. And if the terms that are laid out are not favorable to you, negotiate the contract. It is also your realtor's duty or your real estate lawyer's duty to help you with this, depending on the technicality of the contract.

Here, you all should sit together to discuss your expectations, then he or she helps to communicate your concerns to the seller or the developer.

MAKE A COMMITMENT

After all searches have been concluded and the buyer/investor is satisfied, it is advisable to commit. This involves making a financial deposit to secure your interest, especially if you are looking at a long-term payment plan with a series of instalments soon.

An initial deposit for a property on a long-term payment plan holds a lot of power. It can secure your interest and also hedge your payments against any potential price increase that might occur on the property in the nearest future.

Let us assume you saw a plot of land in an estate in February for ten-million-naira (₦10,000,000) and you are expected to pay one-million-naira (₦1,000,000) monthly in ten (10) months. If along the line the developer/seller increases the price of the estate say, later in April, every subscriber that had keyed in before April would not be affected by the increment. In this regard, you get to earn ROIs even before full payment is finalized on your property.

FINALIZE ALL DOCUMENTATIONS

The last stage of property buying is documentation. All documents should be duly transferred and handed over to the buyer upon full payment.

Documents to look out for in most cases are offer letters, receipts, contracts of sale, deeds of assignment/transfer, and surveys. Note that this is relative and differs from one developer/seller to another.

To further clarify on documentation, if the property purchased has a C of O, the new owner is expected to do a governor's consent.

In real estate law, a C of O is only issued once on a property. Once that property has been sold, the new buyer approaches the government for a governor's consent. This is informing the government that such a property has been transferred to a new owner.

Then on properties that have only excision and gazette, the onus lies on the buyer to apply for the C of O or a governor's consent, especially if the property seller/developer agrees with the purchaser that he or she has no interest in pursuing the C of O.

The obvious fact that real estate could be a capital-intensive venture is enough reason to want to do it right. And that's why caution should not be thrown to the wind when venturing into it. These guidelines aim to ensure that all boxes are checked before you make payments for any property.

CHAPTER 7

RED FLAGS IN REAL ESTATE TRANSACTIONS

"When it comes to property, become a tree without feelings/emotions."

– SM PARANJOTHI PANDIAN

With the presence of dubious people everywhere and how real estate transactions could be porous in Nigeria, it is always advisable to tread carefully while transacting in real estate. The red flags curated in this chapter are mostly to protect the interest of the property buyer. Knowing the large sums of money involved in purchasing real estate, caution should be applied at every stage of the transaction. The red flags to note when getting involved are, but not limited to:

INSPECTION DENIAL

One of the things that inform your buying decision in real estate is inspecting the property in which you have shown an interest. Upon request, if you encounter a denial of access to inspect the property, then this is a big "NO."

A good real estate agent would be glad to take you on an inspection as it is part of their duty. Denying you access to inspect means there is something wrong somewhere. It is either they have no property to offer you, or the parties involved are outrightly dubious.

IMPATIENCE ON THE PART OF ANY PARTY INVOLVED IN THE TRANSACTION

No one should hasten or hurry a real estate transaction. If there seems to be any form of impatience or hastiness from any part of the parties involved, it is advisable to retrace your steps, and either observe and allow more time to pass or back out completely.

Take your time and go at your own pace. However, do not drag for too long in committing, especially if you are comfortable with what you have seen, and all due diligence boxes have been checked. Too much delay could make you lose out on a great offer.

NON-PROVISION OF PROPERTY DOCUMENTS FOR SIGHTING

Every seller should be willing to show you documents that back up their property. Understandably, you cannot be given copies before you make a financial commitment, but they should be available for you to see. In cases of abrupt shielding of documents, know that something fishy is going on there. They are probably either about to pass off someone else's property as theirs, or they are camouflaging someone else's documents for a property that does not belong to them.

AVOIDANCE OF LEGAL CHECKS

As a potential buyer, you have the sole right to "conduct a search" on any property that you intend to buy. In cases of obvious avoidance or where they solely request that someone from their team should search for you, it is advisable to walk away.

REFUSAL TO OFFER EVIDENCE OF PAYMENT

As a purchaser, you are entitled to some form of paperwork after making financial commitments. This could be receipts, acknowledgment letters, offer letters, contracts of sale, and other documents. Documentations and paperwork vary depending on the sellers or developers. What should be consistent here is that all valid documents are in your name. If this is not provided, then it is a noticeably big red flag.

INCOHERENT FIGURES

If all figures presented do not add up, especially when it is intentionally puffed or exaggerated just to attract buyers, then step back and do a proper search. It is advisable to always check the price of properties around the location that you are interested in; just to be clear on what price range to expect. Unless the property itself has amenities or specifications that could make it more expensive than its neighborhood.

MODE OF PAYMENT

The acceptable mode of payment for real estate transactions is either via bank transfers, bank drafts, or cheques (There are people who are wary of cheques because of the processes involved and the obvious fear of it being a dud). Making payments in cash is not advisable.

The goal is to ensure proper accountability and documentation on whichever mode of payment you choose to adopt. Any form of payment that does not allow for proper documentation should not be honored.

UNVERIFIED OWNERS OF PROPERTY

As a potential investor or property buyer, you have the right to see or hear from the seller. Meetings can be physical or virtual depending on the preferred mode, especially in cases where the seller and buyer are not in the same location. This helps you to correlate the seller to any evidence presented by the person or agent intermediating between you and the seller. This is to truly ensure that the seller is the rightful owner of the property being presented.

Note that the only exceptions to this are cases of lawyers with power of attorney to sell properties on behalf of property owners, or if you are buying from an established developer who has put processes in place to aid seamless transactions. In the case of lawyers with power of attorney, ensure to correlate documents provided with proof of power of attorney.

WHEN IT ALL LOOKS TOO GOOD TO BE TRUE

If it sounds too good to be true, it is too good to be true, especially with the prices being offered on the property. Every location has a price range. If it is too low compared to the prices of other properties in that same location, then it is worth looking into. Do not be caught buying a property or a house that you could be spending way more than the cost price to refurbish or fix, unless in cases of distress sales which need to be investigated.

The disparity between the price of a distress sale should not be too far from the price value of houses or properties in that same location. The process involved in purchasing real estate should not be bogus. It should be transparent, seamless, and not tedious. If it feels off and awkward, it is advisable to retrace your steps, investigate, analyze the situation, re-strategize, or walk away.

Again, it is important to note that you are not limited to the red flags discussed in this chapter. Your gut feeling should not be disregarded too. If it does not feel right, it is not right.

Lastly, be willing to spend a few coins on various aspects of due diligence and engage the right team just to be sure that you are getting things done properly. This is the only way to identify some of the red flags that have just been mentioned.

ASSET OPTIMIZATION AND PROPERTY PROTECTION

"Every individual deserves to be educated and
fully informed on the details that go into every
touchpoint of a real estate transaction."

– DOUG FISH

A piece of real estate without a proper optimization and preservation plan could be dead on arrival. A well-optimized real estate portfolio can impact heavily on its returns, monetary value, and overall performance. The goal here is to strike a balance between efficiency, reliability, and longevity of the property that has been purchased. To fully optimize your assets, here are a few things to note:

SEEK TO ENHANCE LIQUIDITY

Being that real estate is illiquid (i.e., an asset that is not easily converted into cash), one key thing to note before even embarking on purchasing any type of real estate is to research the ease of disposal. Can the property at hand be easily disposed of? If not, what are the things that could be done to facilitate its disposal? Enhancing the liquidity of a property could involve a lot. This might entail enhancing the physical features of the property, juxtaposing your prices with other properties around to be sure your property is not overpriced, or re-strategizing your marketing/promotion plans.

SPREAD RISKS

Real estate is not averse to risks. It is always advisable to spread one's risks when it comes to investing in real estate. The best way to go about this is to explore different real estate investment options (take a look at the strategies discussed in Chapter 5). Seek to invest in bits across different viable options.

Knowing what works in a location per time is also particularly important. Do not be so vested in residential real estate while the location of your property is calling for commercial real estate. And do not be so carried away with the potential that the short-lease business offers that you completely hold out on long-lease investments.

The bottom line is to spread your risks across different asset classes to get the best out of your investments. It is always important to "read the room" and know what would work effectively per time.

UNDERSTAND REVENUE PATTERNS

Each real estate asset possesses a distinct revenue pattern, which can vary from generating monthly income to annual returns or even one-time gains. It is crucial to comprehend this revenue pattern and the income potential of your assets. This understanding will serve as a valuable guide in determining the most effective approach to position it for sale or management.

SEEK TO UNDERSTAND THE GOVERNMENT REGULATIONS ATTACHED TO THE CATEGORY OF PROPERTY INVOLVED

Regulations like taxes, government levies, and land use act should be studied and well understood. Being knowledgeable on the type of tax or government levies that are due to your property could help plan the activities and use of such property. It also helps to manage the excesses that could be incurred overall.

MANAGE THE COST OF MAINTENANCE

All income-generating assets come with different degrees of maintenance, and real estate is no different. A fundamental part of the factors to consider before venturing into procuring a property is the overall cost of maintenance. Even after making a purchase, the issue of maintenance would always pop up. The goal here is to ensure that the cost involved in maintenance is reduced to the barest minimum to optimize profit.

GET INSURANCE ON YOUR REAL ESTATE ASSET

There are insurance policies for property and homeowners. The insurance policy aims to protect property owners in the event of incidents like natural disasters. A typical example could be fire incidents and other property damage that might occur from theft and other unforeseen circumstances. See a real estate insurance policy as a protection for your assets.

GET AN ESTATE PLAN

Protecting your asset in this regard goes beyond insurance policies. Here we liken "protection" to having an "estate plan." This is a strategy that involves one still being in control of their real estate assets even after their demise.

It is worthy of note that the title "next of kin" does not hold water in the event of the demise of an asset owner. An estate plan is provided by asset protection services, and it contains several types which investors can explore. Examples include a living trust, probate (i.e., a will) and so many others. We would be dwelling more on the most common one: a will!

The mere thought of writing "a will" is quite scary, but what is scarier are your loved ones having to lose all that you have labored for, or your property getting into the wrong hands and being mismanaged. A will appropriates and apportion bits of every asset in one's portfolio to the right hands with the sole aim of fostering management and enabling smooth transfer to beneficiaries without unnecessary court procedures.

Please note that "God forbid! Death cannot happen now" is not a strategy. What is worse than not having a protection plan in place is having one's entire legacy and assets completely go to waste, because it got into the wrong hands.

It is imperative to note that without optimization and protection strategies, the efforts put into property acquisition may be useless. And this is because protection strategies are the only true way to preserve the value of real estate properties. To safely effect this, it is always advised to adopt a combination of different preservation strategies that have been discussed in this chapter.

The overall end goal is to ensure that every real estate asset is fully optimized and protected. And to achieve this, all protection and preservation strategies should be imbibed with prudence and a good sense of judgement.

CONCLUSION

"When you invest, you're buying a day
that you don't have to work."

– AYA LARAYA

Will Rogers once said, "Don't wait to buy real estate; buy real estate and wait."

It is worthy of note that **real estate is not a get-rich-quick scheme, neither is it gender, or age biased. Real estate can be ventured into irrespective of age, gender, or social stratum.**

Real estate has been recorded to be one of the world's most valuable assets with the capacity to unlock so many doors to financial freedom. This attribute should not be underestimated if sustainable wealth is of great priority and interest to the reader.

There have always been questions surrounding the profitability of Nigerian real estate and how to safely invest and buy properties without getting burnt. "HOW TO INVEST AND PROFIT FROM THE NIGERIAN REAL ESTATE MARKET" seeks to answer these questions. Not only does it answer questions surrounding profitability but also goes ahead to prove that real estate transactions could be very flexible if the right approach is deployed. It further strives to identify different viable and sustainable strategies to guide anyone seeking to succeed as an investor in the real estate space. These proven and sustainable methods, if carefully followed, promises remarkable success.

Money, they say, is no respecter of man: *"The way you treat the money in your hands today will determine, to a large extent, how money could treat you in the nearest future."*

This game called "real estate" holds exciting opportunities with so many possibilities for everyone. You should not be a spectator; rather, be a skillful PLAYER on this field and reap the immeasurable rewards inherently!

SEE YOU AT THE TOP!

REFERENCES

Chen, J. (2019, May 2). Real Estate: Definition, Types, How to Invest in It.
Investopedia. https://www.investopedia.com/terms/r/realestate.asp

Bitton, D. (2023, January 20). What Is A Triplex | Definition & Examples. *DoorLoop*.
https://www.doorloop.com/definitions/triplex

*real-estate noun - Definition, pictures, pronunciation, and usage notes | Oxford
Advanced Learner's Dictionary at OxfordLearnersDictionaries.com*. (n.d.).
https://www.oxfordlearnersdictionaries.com/definition/english/real-
estate?q=real+estate

*landlord noun - Definition, pictures, pronunciation, and usage notes | Oxford
Advanced Learner's Dictionary at OxfordLearnersDictionaries.com*. (n.d.).
https://www.oxfordlearnersdictionaries.com/definition/english/landlord?q=l
andlord

Reporter. (2022, August 7). 10 reasons you should invest in real estate. *Tribune
Online*. https://tribuneonlineng.com/10-reasons-you-should-invest-in-real-
estate/

Okonkwo, I. (2022, October 7). How real estate remains the hedge against
inflation. *Businessday NG*. https://businessday.ng/real-estate/article/how-
real-estate-remains-the-hedge-against-inflation/

Chen, J. (2021, March 22). What Are Real Assets vs. Other Asset Types? *Investopedia*. https://www.investopedia.com/terms/r/realasset.asp#:~:text=Real%20asset s%2C%20like%20financial%20assets,which%20are%20its%20intangible%20a ssets.

Emeh, J. (2022, December 12). Femi Otedola's net worth and source of wealth. *Clacified*. https://www.clacified.com/business/16/femi-otedola-net-worth#:~:text=Femi%20Otedola%20has%20an%20estimated%20net%20wort h%20of%20%241.8%20billion.&text=Femi%20Otedola%20is%20among%20th e,an%20importer%20of%20fuel%20products.

WSS Author. (2022, January 6). Mcdonald's Real Estate: How They Really Make Their Money. *Wall Street Survivor*. https://www.wallstreetsurvivor.com/mcdonalds-beyond-the-burger/

Carmart Blog. (2023, January 28). Kennedy Okonkwo Net Worth, Cars, House, And Biography – Nigeria Real estate mogul. *Carmart*. https://www.carmart.ng/public/blog/about-kennedy-okonkwo/

Tognini, G. (2021, October 5). The Richest Real Estate Billionaires On The 2021 Forbes 400 List. *Forbes*. https://www.forbes.com/sites/giacomotognini/2021/10/05/the-richest-real-estate-billionaires-on-the-2021-forbes-400-list/?sh=783d908e6324

Apodaca, P. (1998, May 14). Billionaire Developer Weds - Los Angeles Times. *Los Angeles Times*. https://www.latimes.com/archives/la-xpm-1998-may-14-me-49656-story.html

Capitalism.com. (2023, January 17). Grant Cardone's Net Worth and How He Got Rich in Real Estate. *Capitalism.com*. https://www.capitalism.com/grant-cardone-net-worth/

Entrepreneurs.Ng. (2019, October 4). Allen Onyema – Biography, History And Businesses Of An Uncommon Patriotic Citizen. *Entrepreneurs.Ng*. https://www.entrepreneurs.ng/allen-onyema/

Bromley, V. (2016, July 24). What is Property Development? - Property Development - Medium. *Medium*. https://medium.com/the-property-developer/what-is-property-development-2c82464efdee

Davies, B. (2023). Sizes of lands in Nigeria Explained - Plots, Acres & Hectares. *Nigeria Property Centre*. https://nigeriapropertycentre.com/blog/general/sizes-of-land-in-nigeria-explained-acres-a-plots

Nwachukwu, I. (2022, October 27). How To Start A Short-Let Business In Nigeria. *Connect Nigeria*. https://articles.connectnigeria.com/how-to-start-a-short-let-business-in-nigeria/amp/

Tross, K. (2023, January 6). 8 Benefits of Joint Property Ownership. *Pacaso*. https://www.pacaso.com/blog/8-benefits-of-joint-property-ownership

Square Blog. (2023, February 28). Nine Factors that Influence Real Estate Values. *Square Yards*. https://www.squareyards.com/blog/nine-factors-that-influence-real-estate-values

Tahir, M. (2021, February 16). The Effects of Government Policies on Real Estate Sector. *Graana.com*. https://www.graana.com/blog/the-effects-of-government-policies-on-real-estate-sector/amp/

Ogundepo, J. (2021, November 13). 10 things to consider before buying a house. *Punch Newspapers*. https://www.punchng.com/10-things-to-consider-before-buying-a-house/%3famp?espv=1

IfeOluwa, A. (2021, April 24). 5 Real Estate Transaction Red Flags. *Land Sprout*. https://landsprout.com/5-real-estate-transaction-red-flags/

Forsyth, E., & Grimsley, S. (2022, February 27). Dishonest Behaviour In Real Estate. *Study.com*. https://study.com/learn/lesson/dihonest-behavior-real-estate-fraud-puffing-misrepresentation.html

Osonuga, F. (2021, March). What To Know About Land Titles In Nigeria and How They Impact Your Property. *THISDAYLIVE*. https://www.thisdaylive.com/index.php/2021/06/22/what-to-know-about-land-titles-in-nigeria-and-how-they-impact-your-property?amp=1

Clifford, C. (2017, March 27). How this self-made millionaire went from janitor to real estate mogul, outselling the pros 100-to-1. *CNBC*. https://www.cnbc.com/2017/03/27/self-made-millionaire-went-from-janitor-to-real-estate-mogul.html

Aoki, K. (2021, April 5). What influences a property's value? *finder.com*. https://www.finder.com/what-influences-a-propertys-value

McLeod, N. S. (2023). 100+ Real Estate Quotes to Motivate You to Invest. *Everyday Power*. https://everydaypower.com/real-estate-quotes/

NaijaHouses. (2022, August 8). Is Real Estate Profitable In Nigeria? *NaijaHouses*. https://www.naijahouses.com/blog-details/is-real-estate-profitable-in-nigeria#:~:text=Final%20Thoughts,with%20little%20to%20no%20investment.

Egole, A. (2022, May 23). Experts canvass real estate's contribution to GDP growth. *Punch Newspapers*. https://punchng.com/experts-canvass-real-estates-contribution-to-gdp-growth/?amp

Agbana, R. (April 5, 2019). How My Shoe Marketing Skills Launched Me Into The Real Estate Business. *Vanguard News*. https://www.vanguardngr.com/2019/04/how-my-shoe-marketing-skils-launched-me-into-the-real-estate-business/amp/

Shobowale, L. (2023, January). Real Estate Key to Sustainable Development. *THISDAYLIVE*. https://www.thisdaylive.com/index.php/2023/01/07/real-estate-key-to-sustainable-development?amp=1

Baker, G., & Strozyk, K. (2022, September). Top 10 Benefits of Investing in Real Estate (+ Possible Cons). *Fit Small Business*. https://fitsmallbusiness.com/benefits-of-investing-in-real-estate/

Adams, R. L. (2019, May 24). How to Make Money in Real Estate: 8 Proven Ways. *Entrepreneur*. https://www.entrepreneur.com/starting-a-business/8-proven-ways-to-make-money-in-real-estate/298748

Sutton, L. S. (2023, February 9). 10 Reasons Why Every Entrepreneur Should Invest in Real Estate. *Entrepreneur*. https://www.entrepreneur.com/starting-a-business/10-reasons-why-every-entrepreneur-should-invest-in-real/444235

Shour, E., & Rohde, J. (2021, December 21). How to protect your real estate assets: 6 strategies to know. *Stessa*. https://www.stessa.com/blog/how-to-protect-real-estate-assets/

Top Real Estate Blog. (2017, December 11). A guide on how to protect your wealth from undesired influence | Top Real. *Amazing Property*. https://amazingproperty.com.ng/blog/a-guide-on-how-to-protect-your-wealth-from-undesired-influence/

The Editors of Encyclopaedia Britannica. (2023, February 14). Skyscraper | Definition, Building, History, & Facts. *Encyclopedia Britannica*. https://www.britannica.com/technology/skyscraper#:~:text=The%20term%20skyscraper%20originally%20applied,than%2040%20or%2050%20stories.

McDonald's Net Worth 2010-2023 | MCD. (2023, May). *MacroTrends*. https://www.macrotrends.net/stocks/charts/MCD/mcdonalds/net-

worth#:~:text=Interactive%20chart%20of%20historical%20net,21%2C%20202
3%20is%20%24213.95B.

Khanna, A. (2023, March 10). 5 Reasons Why Traders Lose Money in the Stock
Market! *Investing.com*. https://in.investing.com/analysis/5-reasons-why-
traders-lose-money-in-stock-market-200570528

ABOUT THE AUTHOR

Adaeze Obikoya is a Property Advisor and Acquisition Specialist. Best known as the Chief Strategist at Sales Vantage Consult Ltd., an award-winning real estate sales and marketing firm in Lagos, Nigeria. She has comprehensive skills and vast knowledge in sales, marketing, and purchase of both domestic and commercial real estate.

Her commitment to transparency and expertise in protecting the interest of all parties involved in business transactions have earned her a continuous array of clients both at home and abroad.

Having worked for a telecommunications company for four (4) years as a customer care executive, Adaeze ventured into real estate sales and marketing in 2017 afterward. She has certificates that cut across entrepreneurial management, realtorship and its ordeal, and customer service from the Enterprise Development Centre of the prestigious Pan Atlantic University and other real estate training programs.

Her educational qualifications include an MSc in Environmental Management & Technology from The University of Manchester, Manchester, United Kingdom, and a BSc in Chemistry from Delta State University, Delta State, Nigeria.

She is married and a mother to two lovely daughters.

Adaeze Obikoya is enthusiastic about making people homeowners and would always lend her voice to anything that contributes to the success stories of real estate. As a crusader of continuous service improvement in the real estate market, she is proud to say she takes away the pain points likely to be encountered when purchasing or selling real estate in Nigeria. Her unique and unparalleled expertise is also exclusively available to guide you through that viable and profitable real estate investment decision.

You can connect with her via these media:

- Email: salesvantageconsult@gmail.com
- Facebook: SVC_Realty
- Instagram: @svc_realty